TOULOUSE
THE STORY OF A
CANADA
GOOSE

By
Priscilla Cummings

*May you never lose
your way!*
*Priscilla
Cummings
2005*

Illustrated by
A.R. Cohen

Tidewater Publishers
Centreville, Maryland

A good October day was like toast, Toulouse liked to say. The edges were crisp, but the middle was soft and warm. Today was such a day, with the sun filling pockets of the cornfield like melted butter. Overhead, a few sleepy clouds stretched across the sky while a gentle breeze rustled the dried cornstalks.

Toulouse welcomed the midday warmth and peace. It had been a long and exhausting trip from Canada this year. Sometimes he worried he was getting too old for all that flying. He was glad the return journey was five months away.

Even at home in northern Quebec, Toulouse often thought of his beloved second home, here in Maryland. For as long as he could remember, he had spent every winter with his family at the same refuge. All except the one, of course.

Toulouse shook off the unsettling memory and carefully folded up his bad leg. To a goose, there is nothing quite so wonderful as a one-legged nap. Toulouse chuckled, recalling his first: "You've got to be kidding!" he had said to MaMa. All she did was smile and say, "Try it, mon cheri."

Just then, Brigitte honked so loud she startled the entire flock. "A story first, Uncle Toulouse! You promised!"

Toulouse sighed and slowly straightened up.

He'd forgotten that he had promised a story. It wasn't that he liked telling stories, but it kept the little ones from sneaking off the refuge while the older geese napped.

"Come on, Uncle Toulouse, we're waiting," Langford whined.

A soft breeze ruffled the black feathers on the sides of Toulouse's head. "All right," he agreed. "I'll tell you a story. I'll tell you *my* story! And maybe you'll learn a lesson, eh?"

The young geese dropped their bills and sucked in their breath. They'd all seen the ugly scars on Uncle Toulouse. But none of them had ever heard the story of what had really happened.

Now Toulouse wondered: Did his tale begin with that first migration south? Or did it actually begin much earlier?

"Ah, yes," he began, "even when I was a little yellow gosling with eggshell still stuck in my damp, new down, I was always rushing off to do things without MaMa's okay, or PaPa's permission. Why, I was just a few hours old one spring day when already I was trying to climb out of the nest . . . "

"Come on, Louise!" I urged my shaky, new-hatched sister. "Let's go exploring, eh?"

Louise blinked and wobbled closer to MaMa.

"How about you, Jean-Louis? Let's see what there is to see!"

But Jean-Louis wanted to be PaPa's favorite son and would do nothing to prompt PaPa's disapproval.

So I sighed and waited for my newest brother, Gaston, to finish pecking his way out of his creamy white shell.

"Bonjour, mon frère! Let's go exploring!"

Gaston opened and closed his tiny bill and stomped his little black feet in the bottom of the nest as though trying on a new pair of boots. "All set!" he announced.

I glanced at MaMa and saw that she was busy plucking down from her breast to reline the nest. Then I checked around for PaPa, but he was down at the pond boasting about his new family.

"Allons!" I whispered in French. "Let's go!"

Quickly, we tumbled over the side of the nest and toddled off into the bushes, bumping into flowers and holding out our stubby, fuzzy wings for balance.

At the top of a small hill nearby, we turned to look back. We saw that our nest was on a hump near the edge of a pond. Beyond our pond, the land was wide, flat, and treeless.

I took a deep breath of the cool air and it felt good. "Do you suppose all of Canada is like this?" I asked Gaston.

He shrugged. He wasn't even out of his shell when MaMa made her welcoming speech so even the name Canada was new to him.

Just then, a loud *ka-ronk!* filled the air.

"MaMa," I said, disappointed.

We were scolded for leaving the nest and ordered into line.

"No time to waste," said MaMa. "You must learn to swim."

PaPa led the way, pausing at the water's edge to look for enemies along the shoreline. When he decided it was safe, he eased himself in. "Come on!" he called. "The water's fine!"

The others hesitated, but not me. No siree! I slid right in after PaPa, pumping my little feet as fast as I could.

"It's easy!" I shouted.

Nearby, another family of geese entered the pond. One of the goslings peered over at me. "Bet I can swim farther than you!" he challenged.

"Bet you can't!" I said.

"Bet I can!"

The gosling lunged forward. I bolted after him.

"Stop!" PaPa called out. "The middle of the pond can be very dangerous!"

"Honk a ronk!" the other gosling's mother called.

But too late. A long, mean-looking fish shot to the surface like a silver streak. A set of jaws opened wide and the razor-sharp teeth of the northern pike glinted with a deadly flash of white. *Kersplash!* Its heavy tail slapped the water!

Then all was quiet. The fish was gone — and so was the little gosling.

"Quickly! Quickly! Back to shore!" PaPa ordered.

I swam until I felt the muddy bottom near shore. Slipping and sliding, I scrambled up the bank and ran to MaMa. Close together we goslings stood, catching our breath and staring back at the pond now so horribly still.

PaPa's eyes were wide, but his voice was calm. "It's the way of the world," he told us.

I was alarmed, though. How could life be so glorious one moment and so frightful the next? I knew it was a warning.

Over the next several weeks, we goslings learned about other dangers in our new world. And each day, MaMa or PaPa taught us something important, such as how to flap-walk quickly on land; how to tip upside down to nibble juicy plant roots from the pond bottom; and how to *listen* for trouble.

"The snap of a twig can be a warning," PaPa emphasized. "All kinds of animals will try to sneak up on you. Fox, mink, wolverines—even snapping turtles."

During this time we changed in appearance as well. Our yellow feathers turned gray, like mud. One day, while tipping at the pond, I noticed yet another difference. "Look!" I burst out. "We've got white cheek patches!"

Jean-Louis searched for his reflection in the pond, but it was impossible to find because the water had been churned into a thousand ripples as I rushed to shore.

"Hooray! *Honk a ronk!*" I sang out. PaPa had said many times that when our white cheek patches appeared it would be time to learn to fly.

That very day we jumped into the air for the first time and felt the rush of wind against our feathers. From high in the sky our pond became nothing more than a blue puddle. Why, a flock of black ducks swimming in the pond looked like a scattering of tiny pebbles!

Now that we were fledglings, every day held exciting new adventures: the first time we flew over the open plains of the tundra! The first time we flew over a herd of caribou!

Summer passed quickly. Almost overnight, it seemed, our world began to change. The reed grass turned from green to brown. A chill clung to the air. Days grew shorter, the nights longer. We began to feel restless without knowing why.

Then, one evening, Uncle Todd showed up with The Map and everyone gathered around our nest near the pond.

"Time we left," Uncle Todd declared.

PaPa nodded solemnly. "I suppose it is."

Together, they unfurled a large birchbark map that was frayed on the edges and looked very old.

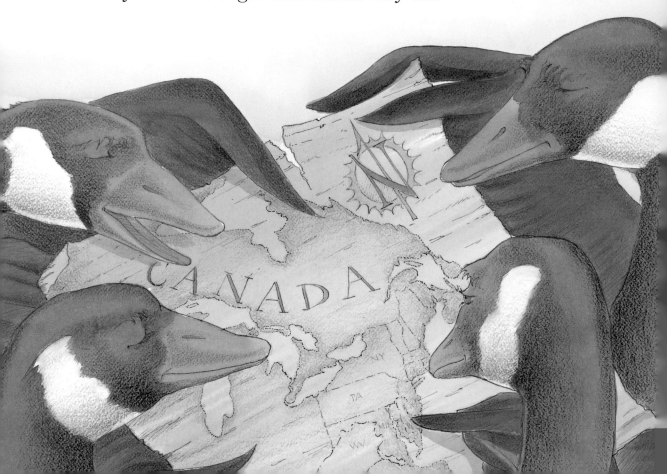

"We'll be taking a trip in the morning," PaPa said, going on to name all kinds of strange places: Hudson Bay, Lake Ontario, the United States, the Susquehanna River.

He swept the tip of one wing over the map. "We'll end up here, at Blackwater Refuge near the Chesapeake Bay."

Everyone in the flock started honking excitedly. Everyone but me. "Why?" I cried out angrily. "Why must we leave?"

Only MaMa saw how distressed I was. "It's because of winter," she explained. "It's too cold to stay here, Toulouse. So we go south, where it's warmer. Just for a few months. We'll return in the spring."

Uncle Todd was rolling up the map. "Don't forget to tell them about the importance of V formation," he reminded PaPa.

"Ah, yes," PaPa said. "We always fly one behind the other in V formation because it saves us energy. The leader, you see, not only points the way, but breaks up the air so it's easier for the others to follow. It's a way of helping each other."

We would fly in V formation? Now *that* sounded like fun. I could really see myself at the front of the flock.

"May I lead first?" I asked.

Uncle Todd chuckled and held a wing over his beak. PaPa smiled. "No, no, Toulouse," he said. "It's only the older birds who lead, eh? You young ones must stay in the rear."

"The whole way?"

PaPa nodded. "It's the way of the world," he said.

I moaned in disbelief.

Early the next day we took off, flying higher and faster and farther than ever before.

"Hey, Gaston! Lookee there!" I called to my little brother. Up ahead, a thin blue line sparkled across the horizon.

"Hudson Bay!" MaMa hollered. "We'll cross it today to get to the western shore where we meet up with the other flocks."

"Magnifique!" I sang out from my place, last in the family V. Such a beautiful sight. And yet, as we flew on our way south, there was only one thing on my mind: leading the flock.

Patience was not one of my virtues, eh? Even at Cape Henrietta Maria, where the Canada geese gathered before the long journey, I ignored MaMa's orders to eat and get myself fat. While the others stuffed themselves on bilberries and crowberries, I was secretly perfecting my take-off so I could capture the lead position.

We stayed at the cape for almost a week and every day more geese flew in. There were thousands of us! One night, as we slept on the water, a loud, raucous honking pierced the quiet night. Jean-Louis swam to PaPa but Louise, Gaston, and I squeezed together against MaMa.

"What's happening?" we cried. "Is it a fox?"

"Calm down," she said. "It's time to go, that's all."

Louise frowned. "Now? In the dark? What about our sleep?"

"Sometimes we travel at night," MaMa said. "Especially when there's a full moon to light our way."

"But how do we know which way to go?" I asked.

MaMa smiled gently. "We follow rivers," she said. "And sometimes the stars help. The one that shines brightest we call the Journey Star."

Uncle Todd hopped up on a flat rock and honked for attention. "Before we leave I want to warn the youngsters about two things: powerlines and airplanes. Now listen up! An airplane roars before it hits! A powerline is silent. So beware!"

Airplanes? Powerlines? There was no way that I was going to lead in the dark with monsters like that lurking around. I went straight to my place in the back and stayed there all night.

We rested by a brook the next day, then repeated the pattern several times, winging our way through the night and resting when the sun came up.

Just before dawn one morning, we crossed a large river and Uncle Todd called out, "St. Lawrence!" Mama honked happily. "We're more than halfway now!" she said.

Soon after, we stopped in a field in the United States to rest and Papa introduced us to a delicious new food called corn. It was on that day, the day of our first corn, that the snow geese showed up.

A hush fell over the field as their shimmering white wings lit up the sky above us. Three times they circled before slowly drifting, like wind-blown lilies, onto the ground below. From the very first, I was awed by their beauty and grace.

I waited for them to come over and share our corn, but the snow geese seemed aloof, sticking to one side of the field.

"Why don't they join us?" I asked PaPa.

He laughed. "Ha! Snow geese mingle with the likes of a common Canada? Don't be ridiculous! It's beneath them, my son."

"But I don't understand."

PaPa shrugged. "No one does, eh? It's just the way of the world. The snow geese go their way, we go ours." He looked me in the eye. "Stay away, Toulouse. Do you hear?"

Just then Uncle Todd honked for attention. "I can *feel* some bad weather coming, possibly an early snow. We'll stay put overnight."

As the geese began to gather in tight family groups, I noticed a solitary snow goose making its way down to the creek.

"Toulouse, you'd better not!" Jean-Louis warned.

"Be quiet!" I hissed, brushing past my brother.

Down at the creek, I planted my webbed feet in the shallow water beside the snow goose and watched as it dipped its bill into the clear running water. I could see that it was young, like me.

"Your first trip south?"

No response.

"I'm from the Ungava Peninsula in northern Quebec. What part of Canada are you from?"

Still no answer. Was the snow goose ignoring me?

"Do you think," I began, "that just because you look like a lily it somehow makes you better than everybody else?"

The snow goose turned its back to me—and flew off!

Well! I wasn't going to let a snow goose think it could fly faster than *me.* Jumping into the air I soon passed the snooty bird with a triumphant honk. But then, the snow goose passed me!

On and on we flew, ignoring all the concerned honking below. Over the field. Over the creek. Over the nearby hills, all the time passing each other furiously. Even when the first icy flakes began to fall, we merely blinked the white stuff out of our eyes and raced on. Uncle Todd was silly to be so worried, I thought. Why, this snow stuff was delightful.

Suddenly, a huge clap of thunder shook the earth. The snow grew thicker and heavier, stinging our eyes and blinding us.

"What's happening?" I cried, trying to turn back.

And then I crashed. I didn't even know what I hit because I couldn't see. In the blink of an eye, the world rolled over. White became black as I plunged into darkness.

Some time later I awoke, cold, sore, and confused. After shaking the sticky snow from my wings I hobbled beneath a nearby hemlock and stood, gazing out between the branches.

"What happened?" I moaned. "Where am I?"

Looking up, I noticed dark lines strung against the sky, like one evil grin after another. Uncle Todd had said we'd *hear* an airplane. Were these the powerlines he'd warned us about? Then, on the ground below, I saw the snow goose, crumpled in a heap. Rushing over, I beat the snow off with my bill. When the goose stirred, I stood back, relieved.

"So," it sniffed, eyeing me and struggling to stand. "*Now* what are you going to do?"

"What am *I* going to do?"

"It's all your fault this happened!" the snow goose insisted. "You'd better get me back before my family leaves!"

Gosh. I wanted to get back, too. But which way to go? The sun wasn't out. Neither was the Journey Star. PaPa had once told us if we ever got lost to listen to ourselves and use our instinct. So I closed my eyes tight and stood quietly. I didn't hear anything, but I had a funny feeling we should fly with the wind to our back. "This way," I said, turning slightly.

The snow goose snorted. "I'm sure you're wrong."

"Fine," I said. "You go your way, eh? I'll go mine."

I was a long way away before I turned to see if the snow goose was following. Sure enough, not far behind, I could see its white wings working their way up and down.

It was hard to fly without someone up ahead breaking a path through the air, without someone to honk encouragement. Before long, I needed to rest. When I landed by a small creek, so did the snow goose. I have to admit I was glad for the company, even if we did sleep on opposite banks and never spoke.

The next morning, as the sun began melting the snow, I stood on the spongy ground studying the sky and wishing I'd listened more closely when Uncle Todd and Papa huddled before takeoff, scratching directions in the dirt.

"We're lost, aren't we?" a soft voice behind me said.

I nodded without turning around.

"We've got to push on, though. There's no choice, is there?"

"Not if we want to see our flocks again," I said.

The snow goose sighed. "If we could just find the Chesapeake Bay."

Excited, I whirled around. "Then your family is heading to Maryland, too?"

"Oh, no. Not Maryland, but Delaware. Bombay Hook. It's a lovely place. The *only* place, really, for a goose—"

"'Tis not the only place for a goose! Maryland is a fine place, too!" I insisted (even though I'd never seen it).

"Well, I certainly didn't mean anything—"

"No, no, I'm sure." I rolled my eyes. Then it hit me and I hung my head. We were both lost and seeking different places.

"Please don't despair," the snow goose said, stepping close. When I looked up, a flash of red-brown fur caught my eye.

"Watch out!" I shrieked, jumping out of the way.

But the fox was quick and pounced on the snow goose, knocking it to the ground. I didn't have time to think about being afraid. Stretching out my wings, the way PaPa had taught us, I ran, headlong and hissing, at the snarling animal.

Startled, the fox leaped back and the snow goose, suddenly freed, took off. I was right behind, those snapping jaws missing me by a feather!

As we gained altitude, the snow goose gulped and glanced over at me. "Thanks."

This time, I said nothing.

Higher and higher we went, finally settling into a path just beneath the clouds. I led, with the snow goose slightly off to my right. After a while we traded positions and the going was easier. The importance of V formation, I thought.

"What's your name?" the snow goose hollered.

"Toulouse," I replied.

"Listen, Toulouse. We can make it. I know we can."

I didn't say so, but I was pleased at this change in tone.

"And by the way," the snow goose called, "my name is Desdemona. But everyone in the flock calls me Dezzy."

"Desdemona?" I had to smile. "Sounds like a girl's name!"

The snow goose giggled. I turned to watch its graceful wings working their magic against the sky. "You're a girl?"

Dezzy just grinned. I felt my face grow warm.

To a couple of young geese on their first migration, a city far below looks like a huge and fearsome monster gripping the land with its concrete tentacles and bright blinking eyes. It even sounds beastly as it clangs and whistles and belches streams of dense smoke. You see, back then we knew nothing of super highways, electric lights, and factory noises.

I was deathly afraid of these cities. But Dezzy finally convinced me we ought to land in one to find out where we were.

"Philly," a pigeon told us. "You're at the Philadelphia Zoo. If you want the Chesapeake Bay you've got to follow the railroad tracks south to Baltimore and hang a left."

We tried to follow those railroad tracks. But the fog was so thick we ended up flying in a circle for two days.

Hungry and exhausted, we hid ourselves in a patch of cattails by a swamp and settled down to rest. For a long time we were quiet. I watched Dezzy's sad but beautiful eyes and could tell she was as homesick for her family as I was for mine.

"Dezzy," I said, "I wondered about something."

She looked up at me.

"You and I seem so much alike. Why is it that snow geese don't like Canadas?"

Her neck straightened and her dark eyes flashed. "Why don't we like you? Why, we've always heard that the Canada geese wouldn't have anything to do with *us!*"

We stared at each other, astonished, then burst out laughing.

"Wait till I tell PaPa," I said. "And MaMa! And little Gaston." But just thinking of my family made me sad again and before I knew it, my laughter had turned into tears.

"Ah, come on, Toulouse," Dezzy said, nuzzling me. "You mustn't give up hope. We'll find our families."

When the weather cleared, we followed the railroad tracks again. But a strange thing happened before we ever came upon another city. A river flowed beneath us and we felt strangely compelled to follow it. It was as though the river was in our blood somehow, leading us on.

We followed the river until it opened up into a huge body of water that stretched wide and blue beneath us. Sunlight danced on the waves below and a million tiny whitecaps flashed in greeting.

Dezzy looked over at me. "Chesapeake?"

"Let's find out!" I nodded to a long, low boat moving slowly through the water. Several sea gulls stood sunning themselves in its cargo bay.

"Hey!" one of the gulls called out as we landed, "I thought you guys travelled in flocks!"

"We do," I said. "In fact, we're looking for our flocks right now. Is this the Chesapeake Bay?"

"Sure is," one gull chuckled. "You guys are all over the place around here. There's the Chester River gang and the crew up on Langford Creek. Why, there's the Choptank and the Blackwater—"

"That's it!" I cried excitedly. "Blackwater Refuge! That's where my family is!"

Just then a dark shadow fell over the barge and all the gulls skittered to one side. We moved out of the way, too, as a large turkey buzzard landed with a heavy thud. His bulky black wings made a big commotion and filled the air with dust.

"Get lost, Turk! This is our barge!" one gull hollered.

But the buzzard didn't budge. "How's that?" he smirked. "Didn't see no sign said 'Sea gulls only'."

I lowered my head so one gull could whisper in my ear: "We call this guy Turk the Jerk because he's always looking for a free lunch. He's taken our food plenty of times."

"Let's go," said one of the sea gulls.

"Yeah," said another. "I don't want to get hit with any more of his bad grammar *or* his bad breath!"

Two sea gulls lifted off. Then three. Then all the rest.

"Wait!" I hollered. "You didn't tell us how to find Blackwater!"

Dezzy and I started to follow but the buzzard stepped smack in front of us. "Just a minute, Goosie Lucies."

As we inched back he kept peering around us, searching for food, no doubt. He sure was ugly, I thought. His beak was too big for his wrinkly, red head and his ragged wings were so enormous that he appeared hunched inside a hand-me-down feather overcoat two sizes too big. He was dusty, too, and smelled *awful.*

"Ain't nuttin' to eat here," he grumbled.

"No, I don't think so," Dezzy quickly assured him.

"Guess I'll have to get me something D.O.R.," Turk said.

We stared at him blankly.

"Dead on the road!" he shouted before laughing heartily at his own joke. "D.O.R.—Get it?"

We cringed as he lifted off, leaving behind a shower of dusty, dirty feathers.

"If you're looking for Blackwater Refuge," Turk called back to us. "It's ten miles thataway."

"Whichaway?" we cried.

But the dumb buzzard didn't say. Instead, he paused and let an air current take him, spiraling, into the sky.

We waited, but he kept circling higher, occasionally rocking and dipping his wings from one side to the other.

"What are you doing?" we hollered impatiently.

"Soaring!" was all he said.

Disgusted, we shook our heads and took off, only to have the buzzard glide down beside us and point southwest with that wretched beak of his. We flew off immediately.

"Careful!" he called after us. "Hunting season on goosie lucies started yesterday."

It was a warning, no? I look back on it now and I realize Turk wasn't such a rotten fellow after all. Just like the humans, eh? Some good, some bad.

Hunting season meant nothing to us and we flew on, excited about being so close to the end of our journey. Soon, we spotted a flock of beautiful Canada geese resting on a pretty little creek. I honked in greeting—Dezzy did, too—as we stuck out our feet for a landing.

Pow! Bam! Ka-Boom! The quiet afternoon was shattered as dozens of shotgun pellets pummelled the air. Several hit me at once, tearing through my feathers into my flesh. I fell with a hard slap onto the pond below and floated, dazed. Dogs barked. Water splashed. And nearby, a wooden decoy bobbed in the rippling water, its unblinking eye staring nowhere.

"So that's where you got those scars, Uncle Toulouse!"
Up until now, Langford hadn't interrupted the story once.

Brigitte whistled. "Wow! How'd you get away?"

"Well," Toulouse continued, "the dogs were far off and
Dezzy wasn't hit, thank goodness. She pulled me by my tail
feathers into the tall reeds, where we hid until the hunters
gave up and left. Later, a kindly duck tended my wounds—"

"Dr. Mallard!" the young geese shouted.

Toulouse smiled. "And we were given food by a most
motherly squirrel—"

"Named Hester!" Brigitte sang out. They all knew Hester.

"What happened next?" Langford asked.

"I ended up staying in Shady Creek the whole winter,"
Toulouse said. "But that's a story for another day, eh?"

"All winter? You must have been so lonely!" Langford
said.

Toulouse thought about that. "Yes," he said, "I missed
my family. But I was busy healing and relearning how to
walk and fly. And I made lots of new friends that winter.
Not just Dr. Mallard and Hester, but Bernie the Sea Gull
and Baron von Heron."

"However," he went on wistfully, "my very dearest friend
remains a snow goose from the west side of Hudson Bay.
She stayed with me, you know. Even after the ground
began to thaw and the first flocks of geese flew overhead
winging their way north, she waited until I could finally fly
again.

"When that day came, we said good-bye and joined
different flocks heading north, hers to Ontario, mine to
Quebec."

"Did you ever see her again?" Brigitte asked.

Toulouse shook his head slowly. "No," he said softly.

Brigitte sighed. "I think you must still be in love with Desdemona, Uncle Toulouse. That's why you never hooked up with a Canada and had a family of your own."

"Don't be silly, Brigitte!" he scoffed. "It's the way of the world, eh? I told you my story so you would learn a lesson. You listen to your parents and maybe *you* won't end up in such big trouble!"

Toulouse winked, and the young geese began to leave. Only Brigitte turned back and noticed a tear in her uncle's eye.

He was thinking, as he lifted his head to the sky, of a beautiful white lily, blown by the wind. The late afternoon sun was still warm. Slowly, Toulouse folded up his bad leg again and tucked himself in for a one-legged nap.